# American
## Public School

# American
## Public School

## Is This Your School District?

## Dennis A. Wallace

authorHOUSE®

*AuthorHouse™*
*1663 Liberty Drive*
*Bloomington, IN 47403*
*www.authorhouse.com*
*Phone: 1-800-839-8640*

*Published by AuthorHouse    02/05/2013*

*ISBN: 978-1-4817-1203-3 (sc)*
*ISBN: 978-1-4817-1202-6 (e)*

*Library of Congress Control Number: 2013901681*

# INTRODUCTION

The American Public School System is an established institution which hits at the heart of the American dream. Whether you love the system or hate it, for the vast majority of America's future generations it is the foundation for launching adult careers. This book centers around the dynamics that determine how that foundation lies. Alas, to many the last few decades of American educational history is a tragedy that has placed the public school system into relative decline against other nations. Many Americans find this decline frustrating when considering the amount of financial deployment made to public schools.

This book attempts to define the parameters of American education by examining the school system's basic building block—the school district. As a reader, you must keep an open mind to benefit from the book's content. Each school district is unique, yet there are common variables found in all American school districts. These all start with the basic relationship of student and teacher. From the beginning of civilization with Adam and Eve, the human element from birth to death always begins with the five senses. The degree to which these senses develop, to include indoctrination in the public school system, is and will always be a combination of one's genes and one's environment.

I will attempt to put the American public school system in a positive light. This is where my book differs from most educational writings today in which you find such strong criticism. I do not so much attempt to state what is right or wrong with the school district as I do to explain the composition of the district. I leave any perspective up to you, the reader, to develop. Any relationship between the district and its employees (all characters in the book are made up) is fictional even though I attempt to pattern this book after a large school district in the Southwestern part of the United States.

Let us begin the journey. I dedicate this book to my brother, Paul Edward Wallace, who passed away on Valentine's Day in 2012. Paul was the second oldest of nine children borne from my mother, Alice Agnes Wallace, who passed from this earth as an angel at the now tender young age of 51 in 1977. May they both rest in eternal peace.

# Chapter One

American Public School is inspired by a true story. Although intended to be a composite of one of 15,000 school districts in the United States, with 90 million students, readers should realize that the current school environment in the country is one of diversity. Complementing the American public school systems are charter schools, private schools, and home schools. The current political debate is on what role federal, state, and local entities should play on the educational landscape in insuring quality student education. This book is not intended to answer that issue, but only to present, sometimes, tongue-in-cheek, what a hypothetical school district in the Southwestern United States might look like.

The Adobe Acres School District (District) and its superintendent, Wally Springs (Springs), strongly controls school policies and positions in the area. Springs' position is the key position in the school hierarchy which runs from the state legislature to the five member school board to the superintendent. He oversees the District's one hundred schools with almost 100,000 students. This includes seventy elementary schools, twenty middle schools, ten high schools, and over 9,000 District employees.

Springs is serving as District superintendent for seven years now since leaving a similar position in Kansas. He sports an excellent public image and strongly controls District policies and procedures. Springs oversees a staff of fifty at the District headquarters which is fondly referred to as Peak Towers (Towers). The major divisions in the Towers include the Administrative Departments which include budgeting and finance, the Cultural Affairs Department, and the Human Resources Department which includes the Substitute Services Section.

Springs micromanages all schools and departments at will and attempts to control District personnel down to the lowliest custodian. He is quick to terminate an employee at the first hint of trouble, basing his actions on a philosophy that an ounce of prevention is worth a pound of cure. He regularly battles the local head of the National Education Union (Union) over its policies and its efforts to support teacher positions that Springs finds to be in conflict with his sound District policies.

Springs tends to ignore legal advice when he disagrees with the school attorney, Abel Adams, which is fairly frequently. His favorite subordinate is Angela Morales (Angela), his vice-superintendent and the daughter of Vicente Morales, owner and editor of the local newspaper, the Adobe Acres Times (Times). The Times is District friendly and prints articles regularly casting the schools in the most positive light possible.

Angela is an excellent example of what Springs likes to see in one of his subordinates. Although she lacks outstanding educational credentials, she is public media smart. Angela was picked over much more experienced applicants because of her background as a media reporter for three years prior to her selection. Angela has the additional advantage of going directly to her father who generally prints Angela's comments verbatim in the Times.

Angela's live in girlfriend, Rosa DeBaca (Rosa), is important to District policies because she is a state lobbyist in educational affairs. She is fresh off a breakup with a previous female companion. As a gorgeous twenty-one year old, Rosa brings sparkle to District events and has been very successful in insuring favorable results for Springs' programs from the state legislature.

# Chapter Two

Budgetary concerns limit the amount of money available for District operations. Springs' focus is on what he sees as quality education which he channels through weekly comments to Angela and then presentations in the Times. Springs also manages to obtain significant grant money from government sources friendly to the District and sources that wealthy educational contributors have been willing to share.

Springs has been called "Magic Wally" because of his innate ability to obtain District funding. His motto is "where there's a will, there's a way." Springs' focus on quality student success is so credible to the outside public that he has been able to direct funding to student development that has other school districts salivating. Periodic articles in the Times adds to the general perspective that Magic Wally is truly magic.

The District Cultural Affairs Department is an outgrowth of the importance of the Spanish culture in the Southwest and is influential in obtaining private and governmental funds. Emilio Rodriquez (Emilio), a Mexican immigrant who came to the United States at the age of six, heads the Department. Emilio works closely with Springs to obtain federal subsidies related to Spanish language learning and has a high success rate.

Emilio has a eighteen year old wife which has drawn criticism from multiple sources, although Angela keeps this potentially explosive story out of the Times. His wife, Maria, was impregnated in Juarez, Mexico, by Emilio's first cousin, Jose, who died in a car wreck three months prior to his baby's birth. Emilio, in an effort to preserve the family reputation, brought Maria to the United States and married her. This family seems insanely happy.

Emilio supervises 14 employees. He requires all of his employees to be fluent in Spanish with a working knowledge of English. The Cultural Affairs Department's major annual program is termed the English Fluency Examination. All students in the District who claim English as a second language are tested to determine their English capabilities in speaking and writing English. Records of improvement are kept for annual progress. Students who fail to show progress from year-to-year receive special tutorial training.

The Cultural Affairs Department is a hotbed of District rumors. Springs attributes these rumors to stereotypes of Latinos and Mexican immigrants. Emilio requires that all subordinates complete a daily journal listing activities in one hour increments. Employees are further required to document any trips completed outside of the Towers. Only one embarrassing incident, involving two coworkers caught in pari delicto, has occurred in the past two years. Angela was successful in keeping this incident out of the Times.

# Chapter Three

Becky Snodgrass (Becky) oversees the Human Relations Department. She is known throughout the District as a sixty year old lady on steroids. Employees in her arena refer to Becky as the "Iron Lady." Springs loves her attitude and often meets with her mornings for a cup of coffee and a review of current personnel issues. They consider employee performance throughout the District and take special notice of specific employee progress and activities. Periodically, Angela is brought in to create a positive story about school success stories. A recent slogan termed "consider the potential" has brought significant attention.

Roberta Garcia (Roberta), a former elementary school principal from Winslow, Arizona, manages the Substitute Services Division under Becky's supervison. She generally has 200 substitutes available in her Subpick system. With two able assistants, Roberta is responsible for insuring that each District teacher's classroom is covered in the event of a teacher absence. The Subpick system is fully automated and each teacher must electronically enter each day and half-day to be missed. The school principals, working through their secretaries will manage other staff absences.

The Administrative Department is divided into three sections. The first section is the special staff which is overseen by Angela and includes counsel, public relations, and special staff. The second section is payroll which has ten employees, and the third section is budget and accounting which controls and audits District spending. Herman Whitewall (Herman), a computer nerd of the first magnitude, is chief of the third section. Herman is Angela's first cousin and Roberta's favorite employee. Like her, Herman considers forty hours to be a good start for the workweek.

Herman is married to a former District middle school teacher, Emily, who treats him like a child. Emily believes that Herman lacks the common sense to tie his shoes straight. She nags him endlessly to the point that Herman stays at work just to escape her control over him. He is an excellent computer technician and highly prized by Springs and Angela who believe that he can fix any computer glitch.

Joanna (Joanna) Sommers is the payroll guru. Although she is 72 years old, she retired from a school district in the Texas panhandle prior to moving to the District. She had been advised that she was just too old to work while in Texas despite 35 years of excellent service. Joanna then scrutinized the want ads for six months prior to finding the payroll supervisory position at the District. She met with Roberta and Springs who insisted that she first undergo a thorough physical before hire. Joanna passed the physical easily, the doctor advising her that she had the physical attributes of a forty year old.

Springs values age and his oldest employee is in special services. Bertha Brooks (Bertha) is in charge of recruiting despite her 77 years age. Angela often advises Springs that he should retire Bertha for health reasons. Bertha has been a heavy smoker for most of her life and weighs over 300 pounds. Springs responds that Bertha would rather die than retire and that she is good for recruiting on the basis that if she can work for the District, anyone can.

Bertha is known as the "cat lady" She occupies an old white house with a decaying picket fence in the center of the city where she houses twelve cats. Bertha allows the cats to roam the neighborhood freely during the day and then plays with them at night. She claims that the cats are great for her recruiting success because their personalities invigorate her efforts.

# Chapter Four

The District is spread out over fifty square miles. Elementary schools (kindergarten through the fifth grade) are spaced out in half-mile quadrants with the higher income schools in the northeast section (Northeast). The southwest section is populated by lower income families and is referred to as the valley (Valley). Middle schools (sixth grade through eighth grade) and high schools are distributed throughout the District by population. High schools are named after United States presidents.

Sandia Middle School is considered a national blue ribbon school and is located in the District's far northeast section. This state of the art school, with an interactive whiteboard in each classroom and a computer assigned to each student receives a federal subsidy as well as strong parental financial support. The District holds a lottery each July to determine the student body makeup. Parents throughout the District are allowed to enter this lottery, but most entrants come from the Northeast.

Of the ten District high schools, there are five general high schools, two vocational high schools, two honors high schools, and one alternative high school. Adobe Acres Alternate High School students include single and pregnant mothers, students with criminal records, and students suspended from other District high schools. This school is a last chance for District students to obtain a regular high school diploma. Graduation rates run at about forty percent.

Among the five general high schools Barack Obama High School, kingpin of the Valley, has an enrollment of 4,000 students, 170 teachers, and 100 staff employees. Obama High is first in sports and first in disciplinary problems in the District. Obama High is last in academic achievement among the five general high schools. The building structure of Obama High is very imposing and is sometimes compared to a maximum security prison.

Peak Towers sits in the center of the District. Springs and Angela attempt to control school agendas with tacit support from the District school board. The principals at the District schools are required to submit weekly status reports on employee changes, budgetary goals, and student achievement. These reports are reviewed by Springs with a managerial style that would make Queen Elizabeth blush.

Angela has two subordinates to help keep track of the individual schools. Monica Gonzales (Monica), fluent in Spanish and with a Master of Business degree is accountable for the District's 70 elementary schools. Boozer Martinez (Boozer), a former high school state champion quarterback at Obama High, oversees the twenty middle schools and the ten high schools. Boozer is well known at local lounges for his poker expertise and his ability to hold his liquor. Monica and Boozer meet with Angela each week to set weekly objectives.

Springs has discipline as first priority. His core philosophy is a military one of more sweat now, less blood later. Sometimes he sees this as a game of whackamo. As he handles one issue, another pops up, then another. Working closely with Angela, Springs focuses on two links. First is to get the best resolution possible, which often involves terminating an employee. Then to put the best spin possible on the outcome which he depends on Angela to deal with. The two pronged attack has served him well over the years.

The District has a special arrangement with the state office of community development whereby students behaving badly serve community service. This generally involves collecting garbage or weeding some of the grassy areas around the District school grounds. This is a way of giving consequences which is generally supported by the parents. Teachers volunteer their time to supervise the work.

# Chapter Five

Springs believes that if he places general routines in place at the schools, in accordance with federal and state regulations, that the education of students should take care of itself. This includes strong support of common core subjects like math and reading and rubrics which spell out specific standards and details for each grade level and subject matter. He has incorporated procedural requirements into a District student behavior manual.

The No Child Left Behind regulations represent a major hurdle for the District. Springs believes that the testing requirements has not changed the major ingredient for success in the classroom of teacher quality. Effective classroom performance is not an accident. Statistics establish that although yearly test scores have jumped around, quality teachers continue to lead the way to higher scores than their peers. That is, the same teachers whose students perform above average one year will see students perform above average the next.

For individual students, a failure to show adequate yearly progress, or improvement each year, results in remediation through summer school or tutoring when in need of extra help. Springs attempts to stay ahead of the curve by providing tutorial help on what he calls pretests. As a result of this extra effort, with committed quality teachers in reading, writing, and math, the District test scores have ranked in the top quarter of the state for ten years straight.

Springs is troubled by the Individual with Disabilities Education Act (IDEA) which requires states to insure that all public schools provide to meet the needs of students with special needs as defined by law. Under IDEA, schools meet with the parents to develop an individual educational program that determines student placement. Students legally are entitled to a free and appropriate public education and parents may demand, and do, obtain appropriate services.

The huge sums of money spent on special education detract from money to be spent on quality education for the bulk of other students. This partially explains why the United States which is at the top end of per capita student spending is about 20th in the world in student performance. Most countries focus on spending on high achieving students which results in better math and reading scores on average.

Springs is troubled by this skewered funding for special education purposes because he feels to the depths of his soul that that these billions of dollars could be used to hire more quality teachers, provide better classroom technology, and significantly improve the overall District environment. However, given the litigious society and the enormous tort awards provided by American juries, Springs is realistic in providing required services for special needs.

# Chapter Six

There are common core values and standards required for each classroom. These often result in teachers teaching to the test. Teachers fully understand that standardized tests given periodically throughout K-12 grades measures overall school success. Teachers understand that should the District schools fail to meet yearly progress, their jobs may be in jeopardy. Under No Child Left Behind regulations, a school failing to make annual yearly progress for four consecutive years may have teachers terminated and, after five years, may see the school closed or taken over by the state.

Springs is proactive when reviewing standardized test results at each school. At the elementary school level, he requires that Monica meet with the school principal at any school which shows a lack of improvement from one year to the next. The school is then given special tutoring. If that school fails to show improvement the next year, the principal is terminated along with any teachers whose classes score below average. Angela then, with Springs' concurrence, places a highly successful principal and effective math and reading teachers into the school to insure improvement. This has always worked to show improvement.

Boomer has a unique style of management. He first checks with Angela prior to making any material decision. Boomer and Angela jointly meet with any school officials in middle or high school on any termination actions. When a school has below average results on any standardized tests, Angela places the principal on probation. If the school fails to meet annual yearly progress, that principal is generally either terminated or moved to another school. Springs is brought into the situation for final decision if Angela recommends a termination action.

Angela is the glue that holds Peak Towers together. Her personality may be favorably compared to that of Secretary of State Hillary Clinton. However, Angela's relative age of 29 and drop dead looks gives her a significant advantage in her negotiations. A child prodigy, Angela graduated from her university at 19 and was given immediate employment at the local ABC affiliate. Additionally, her connection to her publisher father gives her a public media status that can rarely be matched in any school district.

The relationship between Springs and Angela may also be compared favorably to the ties between President Obama and Secretary Clinton. Springs if 58 and happily married to Joy Springs, the mother of his two teenage daughters. Springs treats Angela as an equal because she has the moxie to objectively make decisions based on the evidence. Rarely does Angela let her subjective feelings get in the way of her decision making.

# Chapter Seven

The District's 70 elementary schools are part of an American system that includes four million students for each grade from kindergarten through fifth grades. Basic subjects taught in these District schools include literacy and math. Students often remain in one classroom throughout the school day. Exceptions include special education classes and the pullouts which may include library, art, music, computers, and physical education. Students generally have a lunch period combined with recess and special assembly periods occasionally throughout the school year.

Principals at each school control the campus environment. Springs allows them some discretion in budgeting. There are some District-wide expenditures for each school. Herman micromanages these expenditures for deviations and reports any discrepancies to Angela. Otherwise, each principal must account for any spending over one hundred dollars per transaction that is not routine and a justification document for each nonroutine expenditure over one thousand dollars.

The principals are a mixed lot. 55 of the 70 elementary school principals are female. Each one is required to have a working knowledge of Spanish. Among these principals, Sophia Gonzales stands out. She is a principal at Three Eagles, an elementary school in Northeast where the PTA is very strong. Julia Hicks, the head of the PTA, is a master fund raiser for Three Eagles. When Sophia needs funds for special school projects, she telephones Julia and she holds a fundraiser to obtain the funds. She has never failed the school.

Across the District, in the Valley, Poncho Vallejas is principal of the overcrowded Painted Hills Elementary School. This school was constructed to hold 700 students, but due to population increases, there are 1100 students currently enrolled. Poncho meets regularly with Angela and Monica to discuss productive changes to the school curriculum. Two years ago the previous principal, Paula Twogoods, was terminated after two consecutive years in which the school failed to make adequate yearly progress. Last year, with strong District intervention and in Poncho's first year, Painted Hills showed significant yearly progress in its test scores.

Poncho is a good friend of Boozer. They often meet at lounges in the District on weekends. This is particularly good for Boozer as Poncho is very serious minded and keeps Boozer out of trouble. In many situations, Poncho has frequently served as the designated driver and the law enforcement personnel in the District know them on a first name basis. Boozer is still glorified as a gifted athlete and a good old boy. The high school students look up to him as a role model and Boozer is careful to maintain, with Angela's help, a good public image.

Another well known Valley elementary school is Joan Rivas. Hector Garcia is the principal, but his vice-principal, Alicia Smith, is the heart of the school. This elementary school is unique in that

Spanish is the first language and English is taught as a secondary language. All teachers have Spanish as a first language and several speak weak English. Amazingly, because the school started with a low testing bar, Rivas Elementary has made adequate yearly progress for the last four years in a row. Hector often sleeps in his office, but as one of Angela's cousins and with Alicia covering, his job is secure.

# Chapter Eight

The bus schedule is very important to the elementary school network and is staggered. This creates a 90 minute difference in starting times as the buses move from the Valley to Northeast. The earliest school schedule starts at 7:30 and the latest start is 9:00. Buses represent a significant budgetary cost to the District. This is particularly true of special education students who require special attention. The average number of riders is most heavy in the Valley where overcrowding is prevalent.

Security guards insure that students entering the campus do so safely. These underappreciated employees work for one hour in the morning and one hour in the afternoon, usually at school crosswalks. There are also speed zones surrounding the campus limiting maximum speed to 15 miles per hour. Security guards are supplemented by educational assistants with early school duties.

The typical school day starts with breakfast which is free to low income families. This usually includes pancakes, eggs, and cereal bars. There is a juice and milk as well. Higher income schools, generally in the Northeast, have an open cafeteria in the morning for hungry students prior to class. Students dropped off early to school may go to the playground where teachers with early duty will supervise them.

After breakfast, students recite the pledge of allegiance. Most District schools recite this pledge in both English and Spanish. A few schools also recite the pledge in Navajo. Then the students recite the six pillars of character which include respect, responsibility, fairness, trustworthiness, and citizenship. Then the principal gives announcements over the loudspeaker with a witty quote such as "the early bird catches the worm."

Literacy occupies the next 90 minutes. District schools use a standardized reading book named Treasures, which contains appropriate reading stories, vocabulary, and comprehension exercises suitable for each grade. There is a special teacher's edition which contains acceptable responses, phonics, and complicated instructions. The quality teachers, with hours of extra effort, absorb these instructions and pass the learning on to the students who then tend to score better on standardized test.

# Chapter Nine

Robin Myers (Robin), a teacher at Los Altos Elementary School in Northeast, is a prime example. She is a graduate of the Teach for America program who stayed in the educational field. Robin graduated with high honors from Georgetown University and was selected to teach at an Indian Pueblo in South Dakota. Angela read a story about her teaching in a national magazine and enticed Robin to come to the District. Her fifth grade classes score well above average on national standardized examinations.

Teach for America is a nonprofit organization which has energized the teaching arena. Founded by Wendy Kopp who first proposed the program in an undergraduate thesis in 1989 at Princeton University, it aims to redress educational inequality by enlisting top college graduates and professionals to teach for two or more years in communities throughout the United States. Like Robin, many of these teachers determine to stay in education and generally their efforts result in above average student achievement.

Kindergarten through third grade are extremely important for students to get a head start. Students who fall behind in reading level at the third grade, where the No Child Left Behind first standardized test is administered, statistically have learning difficulties in the remainder of the K-12 process. Students generally enter kindergarten with significantly different backgrounds at age 5 with many of them veterans of preschool programs. By the end of third grade, they are expected to know the letters of the alphabet and to recite phonics flawlessly. Students should know their numbers and be able to do simple arithmetic.

Recess follows the literacy block for 15 minutes. Each school has a playground full of swings, slides, and monkey bars. There is also a grassy field in which students may play soccer, kickball, or just run around the perimeter. Most schools contain a bank of tether ball poles by which students line up and take turns. There are usually three teachers or educational assistants assigned to watch students. Frequently one or two students will sustain a minor injury and then be sent to the school nurse.

A one hour pullout generally follows recess. There is a rotation among physical education (PE) which is twice per week, music or art, library, and computers. Most students love these classes which are the highlight of the day. PE consists of warm up exercises, games, and track. Popular school games are dodge ball, basketball, and battleship. PE teachers have survived No Child Left Behind cutbacks on the theory that a "sound body makes a sound mind."

Computer classes consist of mind bending exercises specifically geared to increasing math and literacy skills. Occasionally students get free time to engage in fun games such as marble blaster. In some schools, at the principal's discretion, computer teachers are being terminated because of budget cutbacks. In these cases, the regular classroom teacher will supervise the computer class.

Art and music are taught in alternative years because of budgetary concerns. These teachers have discretion in class projects and provide an excellent creative outlet for students. Although given a small budget for supplies, most teachers end up spending their own funds for materials independently. Music games offer a nice break from traditional academics while art projects challenge student creativity and are generally hands on.

Library classes taught by the school librarian focus on encouraging student reading. Each student is allowed to check out one book weekly and is held accountable for its return prior to checking out a new book. Periodically the librarian will introduce students to other media, read to students in the library, or show short films. Schools hold book fairs twice annually to sell books and other related items to raise funds for library supplies.

# Chapter Ten

After pullouts, the students go to lunch in the cafeteria. Schools in the Valley provide free lunches to all students. The remainder of District schools charge students who are not low income a nominal charge, generally two dollars, for their meals or the students may bring a sack lunch to school. If a student is unable to pay for lunch, a cheese sandwich is given to the student free of charge.

After a fifteen minute lunch, which in most schools is staggered by grade level, students have a second recess for fifteen minutes. Then students go back to class for afternoon studies.

First up is Everyday Mathematics for 90 minutes. Although this math includes arithmetic, the creative math exercises challenge the students to stretch their imagination in solving quantitative problems with graphs and shapes. The teacher may also inject math games like Top It along with computer math games and exercise.

Springs stresses as a priority the importance of math to student learning development and makes a system of tutors available to students with learning difficulties. He awards math teachers with recognition when students perform well on the math portion of standardized test.

He points out Silvia Gonzales, Atrisco Street Elementary School, in the Valley as an example. Silvia's third grade classes have shown improvement on the math section of the No Child Left Behind standardized test for five consecutive years.

The next period of the school day is 60 minutes and focuses on science. Springs has initiated a connection with hands on science kits sponsored by Buena Noches Tortillas, a local corporation. There is a yearly science fair in which parent sponsored awards are given to winners at each grade level. Robert Graves, a fifth grade teacher at Joan Rivas Elementary, has a student that has won a blue ribbon for three years straight.

The final period of the day is a rotation period which runs about thirty minutes. This is a flexible block which includes social sciences. Depending on the grade level, social sciences may be history, geography, government relations, or interpersonal relationships. Teachers often use this time slot to complete projects from earlier in the day such as from the preceding science block. Some teachers beef this period up with student reading and writing assignments.

Students welcome the bell at the end of the school day. The teacher will divide the students into three groups. First group is either picked up by parents or siblings, particularly at the lower grade levels, or walk home. Second group, usually the largest of the three, are escorted to buses where duty teachers insure safe bus loading. The third group stays after school for multiple purposes. Some students engage in after school activities which may include sports or homework activities.

Although bussed students usually arrive early at school, they must be quick to catch the afternoon bus home. Bus drivers are generally good shepherds who do an excellent job of minding their flock. There are relatively few disciplinary incidents. However, in 2011 there was a tragic bus accident at Atrisco Street Elementary involving a collision between two buses in which five students were severely injured. This accident led to a change in bus procedure whereby a bus coordinator is required to guide buses to specific parking spots at school.

# Chapter Eleven

There are several other categories of staff members working at the elementary schools. In fact the increase in school staff personnel is the major structural change that separates the school of today from that of the previous generation. The District has double the number of employees per student that it had 25 years ago. This includes the addition of the Cultural Affairs Department. However, it is the addition of additional staff at each District school that has ballooned the employee rolls.

Each District elementary school has an average of twelve staff employees for each group of teachers. This is in addition to the administrative office which includes the principal, vice-principal and secretary. There are multiple educational assistants, speech and occupational therapists, math and reading tutors provided by federal and state grants, a school nurse, and a school counselor. This increase in school staff results in an overall average ratio of nine employees for each student at each school.

The school nurse is a key member of the staff. She generally treats students for cuts and bruises. Teachers keep band aids in the classroom dispensing several each day. For more serious illness, students are sent to the nurse who has very limited capabilities. The nurse can provide ice, but not pills. There are special situations, juvenile diabetes for example, when the nurse can give shots or preordained treatments. The school nurse provides beds for students with elevated temperatures to lay down on until a parent picks the student up.

Speech and occupational therapists make regular rounds to District elementary schools as do social workers. These therapists tirelessly work with individual students on a regular schedule. Periodically they address the entire class on general subjects. Social workers work with low income family students The students generally come from single member or broken homes and the social worker attempts to integrate the parents and school officials together in the child's best interests.

# Chapter Twelve

Springs is a strong believer in tutoring. He requests that elementary school teachers make themselves available for a minimum of an hour each day for literacy and math tutoring. Although this is technically a volunteer effort, teachers who fail to volunteer are duly noted by principals. There are additional tutors, including interested parents and other volunteers, who are also willing to work with students individually. Springs partially attributes the District's excellent performance on standardized tests to these tutoring efforts.

Vice-principals at the District elementary schools also serve as school counselors. The principal depends on his second in command to provide appropriate discipline to teachers, staff, and students. Springs expects these principal wannabes to insure that all school employees are satisfied with their positions. Vice-principals are also responsible for dealing with students' parents and for special school events.

Educational assistants to the teachers are becoming more important at the District. Generally they work in kindergartens and in special education classes. These teacher helpers tend to be low paid and underappreciated. The District requires a high school diploma or equivalent for all applicants. In some cases, with a shortage of substitute teachers, they actually take over the classroom from the regular teacher.

There are other key employees at District schools who are not always recognized. This includes parent volunteers, custodians, and cafeteria workers. Cafeteria workers include both those cooking the food, those serving the food, and those taking the meals count. As famously put "it takes a village to raise a child."

Springs believes that parents should be held fully accountable for student behavior and resulting consequences. In general, his philosophy is that the school will discipline the student while punishment is left up to the parents. If a parent reacts with a remark that the District just does not understand her child, a note is made and the situation investigated. Law enforcement is contacted in any case which potential bodily harm is present.

Springs' micromanagement of the District's elementary school has created some ripple effects. In general, the Valley has vowed to run him out of town, while the Northeast believes that Springs should be elected mayor.

Angela puts special emphasis on the middle schools where she is affectionately known as "babe." The twenty principals, fifteen male and five female, generally use Angela as a conduit to pass their positions on major issues to Springs. Middle school includes sixth, seventh, and eighth grades and is often described in educational circles as the place where "the rubber meets the road." During this time period, students are given more freedom to move about the school and are allowed to choose some of their class subjects.

The District requires that all students take physical education in sixth grade. Springs includes health education within this class to include human sexuality. His basic philosophy is that abstinence, though an important part of this subject matter, is not realistic in today's social environment. The human sexuality course includes human anatomy, reproduction, male and female emotional makeup, sexual intercourse, and important physical aspects of life.

The middle school principals are all former teachers who worked their way up to the top school position. Mario Ortiz, principal at Northeast's state of the art Whispering Willows Middle School, is chief spokesman for these principals. Mario meets with Angela weekly to update her on middle school concerns.

# Chapter Thirteen

The basic curriculum is the same in all of the middles schools with emphasis on literacy, math, and science. As in the elementary schools, teachers are requested to volunteer a minimum of one hour per day for tutoring. Toward the end of the eighth grade year, students are given a standardized test to evaluate their preparedness for high school. Students who score poorly on this test are required to attend summer school prior to high school enrollment. Gangs are essentially nonexistent in the District. However, an affiliate of the Crips, which is headquarters in the Los Angeles metropolitan area, has periodically attempted to infiltrate several middle schools in the Valley. Angela is first point of contact on suspected gang activity. Springs' overall policy is that any student caught participating in any gang related activity will be automatically suspended from school.

Among middle school teachers, seventh grade math teacher Merette Oganisis, currently at Dennis Ross, is a legend. Merette has 37 years of teaching experience and was once named national teacher of the year. She is also a former Ms. New Mexico and has a black belt in karate. Many of Merette's students have gone on to brilliant careers to include two governors, one senator, and over fifty teachers.

District middle school classes include six one hour periods and one thirty minute lunch. Additionally, there is a fifteen minute homeroom period just prior to the start of first period in which students recite the pledge of allegiance and the principal provides announcements along with encouraging comments to provide a positive start to the school day.

Courses in literacy, math, and science are required at all three grade levels. Springs has initiated additional required courses in geography and physical education. Most students take an American history course as well. Elective courses are available in homemaking, economics, drama, shop, keyboarding, and band. Principals may petition Angela for other elective classes if they can establish sufficient student interest.

Each District middle school provides thirty minutes for lunch. Half of the students eat lunch in the cafeteria while half bring sack lunches or eat pizza at school provided alternative locations. Students may also purchase energy drinks, candy, or popcorn. Some middle schools worried about student health have requested that the District change its policies on lunch and provide healthy alternatives. Angela has yet to approve any changes.

Middle schools schedule student wide conferences monthly with guest speakers. These hour long conferences bring community guest speakers into the school to encourage students and to provide realistic assessments of future life activities. Guest speakers include celebrities, government officials, and sometimes teachers or other educators. These role models are considered important in providing real life experiences to students.

# Chapter Fourteen

All 20 of the District middle schools have active sports programs. Soccer and basketball competitions are the most popular. The schools are organized into four divisions of five teams each. Each school plays each other division team twice and then the four division winners enter a playoff. The final winning school receives a large trophy to display in glass cabinets in the lobby of its middle school.

West Sandia Middle School in the Valley bills itself as the "beast of the mesa." Its basketball coach, Jose Villas, has won the District championship for three consecutive years. Coach Villas, a former teammate of Boozers' on two state championship teams, teaches his student that "winning is not everything, it's the only thing." This philosophy has caused him some problems with Angela in which Boozer has successfully intervened.

Middle school curricular activities include school plays, orchestra, and band. There are also club activities in Spanish, chess, and music. Students receive their first exposure to musical instruments in middle school. The boys prefer guitars and drums, the girls prefer horns. The 20 schools have a musical festival twice per school year at which individual the District provides individual awards.

There is an annual District drama. Each of the middle schools encourage students in drama to try out. Drama teachers from District high schools select final performers. The drama is presented at the local civic center in front of Springs and Angela and the general public with significant local exposure.

Helen Hayes Middle School is set aside for special education students. The various types of special education programs include those for the emotionally disturbed, those for the physically severely disabled, those for autistic students, and those for the educationally challenged. The size of special education classes is generally limited to no more than ten students. Teachers are required to have special certifications. There is at least one educational assistant in each class.

The District spends four times the amount of money per student in special education classes than in mainstream classes. The Unites States spends over $25 billion per year on these students under No Child Left Behind dictates. Much of this money is for physical disability equipment and special transportation requirements. Springs understands the need for these programs, but laments not being able spend these District funds on other students.

Discipline is a constant problem at District middle schools. Students will text each other at every opportunity, listen to music on Apple products, or socialize if possible. This mixed environment is where students grow into young adults and young men start noticing young women. District policies require that teachers report any incidents of unwarranted physical contact between students to middle school administrators for further investigation.

There are middle school teachers who behave more likes friends to students than mentors. One is the cool Dean James, a 25 year old drama teacher at Dos Rios Middle School in the Valley. James rides a Harley motorcycle to school each day and spends his lunch hour with his favorite students. James, a graduate from Colorado State University, starred in several lavish productions there. He coordinates dramas among the District middle schools.

Marilyn Bridges, an eighth grade social studies teacher at El Sol Middle School, shepherds her best students on an annual spring field trip to Washington, D.C. In addition to visiting the Smithsonian museums, these students visit the White House, the Capitol Building, and the Library of Congress. These students generally meet with the District congressman.

The District middle schools schedule a combined spring dance each year. Students contribute five dollars each to attend and parents volunteer to assist teachers for security purposes. Dance organizers obtain enough funding to hire a popular local band and for refreshments. There has never been any significant trouble at this dance, partially because the dance terminates at 10:00 pm each year.

The District does have serious crime on occasion. Recently, at Marion Roses Middle School, Principal Mark Brooks was terminated from his duties for white collar fraud. Brooks was found to have been using the school's discretionary budget for personal purposes to include the unauthorized purchase of Apple Computer products among supplies artificially listed for school classrooms.

The District sets aside the Heritage Middle School in the Northeast for its honor students. This school offers the same curriculum as the other nineteen middle schools, but accepts a limited number of students nominated by elementary school principals at the end of fifth grade promotion. Principal Mary Hodges, working closely with Angela, makes the final selection attempting to balance factors starting with academic potential. Additionally, some sixth grade students are allowed to transfer in each year if appropriate criteria are met.

# Chapter Fifteen

The District has ten high schools. There are five general high schools, two are vocational technical, two are academic, and one is an alternative high school. Richard Nixon and George Washington High Schools accept students who meet minimum academic requirements although students from Heritage Middle School are automatically admitted to Richard Nixon. George Washington High School is located in the Valley.

District high schools run from ninth through twelfth grades. The five general high schools provide a broad variety of classes without emphasis in any particular subject. Although students are required to take certain mandatory subjects to include four years of English, four years of mathematics, three years of science, three years of social sciences, and two years of physical education, a significant percentage of subjects are electives.

District electives include athletics, performing arts, music, computer related subjects, foreign languages, shop, home economics, and ROTC. Springs will also provide an elective if a group of students petition for one and can find a qualified teacher. Students may also take advanced placement classes, which are standard at the two academic high schools, and may even coordinate with other area high schools and colleges under special circumstances.

All ten high schools begin at 7:30 am. There are seven class periods which includes one study hall. Students are provided one hour for lunch with eleventh and twelfth graders allowed to go off campus. There is a small cafeteria at each school and several snack bars which serve pizza, hamburgers, hot dogs, and health foods. In going with the modern trend, Springs does not allow soda or candy on the high school grounds. Bottled water, milk, and juice drinks are readily available.

Each high school has a multitude of after school activities. Athletics are most popular among students but any group of students may petition to start a club. There is a strong Spanish Club, a Chess Club, a Bike Club, at Adobe Acres Vocational High School, a Future Farmers of America Club, and at Richard Nixon High School, a Socrates Club. George Washington High School English teacher Miles Stanton recently started a Dead Poets Society Club, patterned after the movie of the same name.

The two vocational high schools prepare students for career and technical occupations. This includes agricultural and technical trades to include cooking, mechanics, and various shop related positions. Students with valid driving licenses are allowed to take truck driving classes with parental consent. Interestingly, Jacob Sparks, a high school graduate with no college credits, teaches the driving classes. Springs has successfully obtained sponsors locally to pay for many of the expenses incurred for equipment at the vocational schools.

Dwight Eisenhower Career High School has special classes in computer courses and secretarial sciences. Springs has obtained state of the art computer and related equipment from Dell Computers. Many of the twelfth graders at Eisenhower have secured excellent positions with local businesses on graduation. Given the current high unemployment situation for youths in the United States today, Springs considers this school a success story.

U.S. Grant Alternative High School is located in the heart of the Valley. The student body of 800 varies significantly over the school year. This "last chance" high school serves single mothers, pregnant young women, and a mixture of students who have dropped out of the other nine District high schools or been suspended because of disciplinary problems to include minor crimes. A minority of students, primarily young women, actually obtain a high school diploma while the others, primarily troubled young men, drop out.

Springs stresses sports competitions among the ten high schools. The five general high schools field teams in football, basketball, baseball, and soccer. All of these sports raise revenue for the District and lead to intense state competitions. Barack Obama High School has a large number of trophy cases and is generally considered the District high school team to beat. William Jefferson Clinton High School in the Northeast is Obama's major competitor.

Although Nixon and Washington High, along with the two vocational and one alternative high school (which generally joins Adobe Acres Vocational School as a joint team), participate in these major sports without much success, the other athletic sports teams are optional at each school. For example, all schools have cheerleading, but only the five general high schools have track, tennis, wrestling, and swimming teams. Both academic high schools have chess teams which compete state wide.

Springs has initiated a series of academic competitions among the schools to include music, public speaking, math and science, and literacy contests. These District events are generally sponsored by national and local businesses and involve significant awards to include trophies and blue ribbons. Springs is very successful in obtaining funding primarily because of the hard work and media capabilities of Vice-Superintendent Angela Morales.

# Chapter Sixteen

Among young women, cheerleading is becoming an extremely popular sport. Young women in particular seek the Spring tryouts. District success leads to state and national competitions later on. The District schools participate in a two week summer camp just prior to the beginning of the new school year. Amazingly, U.S. Grant Alternative School has won the past three year competitions under Alicia KIm's coaching expertise. Alicia graduated from the alternative school five years ago and went then went to the University of New Mexico to obtain a physical education degree, serving as captain of the UNM cheerleading squad.

ROTC is popular at the five general high schools. Colonel Juan Gonzales is the District's lead instructor and supervises all five of the ROTC programs. Colonel Gonzales is physically located at Obama High School which provides Air Force ROTC as an option. There are usually two students each year who graduate and go on to the military academies. John Stevens, a former student from

Nixon High School graduated last year as the top honor student at the Naval Academy in Annapolis, Maryland.

District school climate varies among the high schools. Students at the academic high schools generally have more freedom to move about the campus. Sandra Smith, a Stanford University graduate, is a popular math teacher there. She has collaborated nationally on a new Algebra textbook and serves on several national academic committees. Sandra's students score the highest in math on District standardized testing and win most District math competitions.

The two academic high schools provide a strong array of AP classes, but leave room for special elective classes and interaction between students and teachers. When not in class, students are much more likely to chatter with the teachers and administrators. Unlike in the other high schools, it is cool to be smart. Standardized test scores tend to average about 25 basis point above the average for the other eight schools and in the new rating state rating system for all public schools, both Nixon and Washington receive strong A's.

At Washington High School, John Lovato is the senior English teacher. John is one Springs' best friends and a popular teacher among students keen on literature. He teaches twelfth grade English and instructs a seminar class with a limited number of students each Spring. During Spring break, at student expense, he shepherds his students to Mexico City, Mexico, to study Mexican literature.

At Obama High School, Jorge Sandoval, a Spanish teacher, is well liked. At the age of six, Jorge's parents crossed the Rio Grande with Jorge and ten brothers and sisters. Fortunately, the Sandoval family ended up in Hatch, New Mexico, on a chile farm where they were all adopted by an older couple suffering from an empty nest syndrome.

Jorge worked hard as a youth and then went to New Mexico State University. After two years with Teach for America, Jorge selected Obama High in order to help other immigrant children integrate into America.

Springs has the final veto on all hiring of teachers and staff. Angela and Boozer will provide him with recommendations, but because there are so many potential personnel actions, he usually only involves himself with special circumstances. Working closely with Angela, Springs has a keen interest in the Teach for America program and actively seeks out teachers who are completing their two year requirements. Springs also seeks out teachers with alternative teaching credentials because he appreciates their real life experiences.

One recent alternative teacher recruit, Xiomara Meesh, is a legend at Adobe Acres Vocational High School. She teaches the culinary arts after a twelve year career at General Mills in Minneapolis, Minnesota. Xiomara is nicknamed "Betty Crocker" by her students. Her classes are so popular at Eisenhower that students must apply for a special selection process. Students who graduate are actually sought out by major American food companies for employment.

# Chapter Seventeen

Grant Alternative High School is sometimes referred to as the zoo. Springs personally selected its principal, Emma Thompson, after an exhaustive search. Emma is a fifty year old former English teacher from Lexington, Kentucky, who is legally blind in both eyes. She is an energetic and amazing lady who is dearly loved by the young women at the high school. Emma is also considered by the alternative school's teachers as an ideal mentor. Most people are genuinely surprised at this until they actually meet her in person.

Emma pushes the basics at Grant. There are few electives and students realize that this is their last chance to get a high school diploma. The young men, having failed at other high schools, tend to lack motivation and the majority of them wash out. The single mothers and other young women are split in two. Many of them, like the young men lack motivation and eventually wash out. The second group of young women, particularly the single mothers and those pregnant, may have been excellent students at the other schools. They work hard and some of them go on to college and promising careers despite early motherhood.

Grant High has a relatively strict disciplinary policy. Students are suspended or terminated for a variety of misdemeanor activity to include fighting, sexual harassment, and drug use. Emma may be a mother hen to the young women, but she does not tolerate gateway drug use and will quickly terminate anyone found smoking pot. The young women understand this policy and, with loss of a state of the art day care center looming, most are careful to avoid this trouble and will report any other student not in compliance.

Victor Lyons is the assistant vice-principal at Grant. The students refer to him as the sheriff. Victor is a deputy sheriff who works at local sporting events when not at school. He is very strict with the young men at the school and has a low tolerance for fighting. He is well liked by both Springs and Angela and his recommendations are generally followed by Emma when requested.

Both Emma Thompson and Victor Lyons attempt to maintain a regular high school environment at Grant. There are District sports competitions and Grant has excelled in cheerleading competitions. There are a few extracurricular activities besides the sports programs. One popular activity is the homemaking club which the single mothers enjoy and find useful. This club has excellent sponsorship among local businesses and the young women members make weekly field trips.

Nonetheless, Grant gets strong District scrutiny because of its last chance status and the administrators, staff, and teachers are well aware of its student statistics. Standardized test scores tend to be significantly below the District average. Security is much tighter than at the other District schools and students are regularly found smoking in unauthorized areas and occasionally engaging in sexual activity. Springs, however, is pleased with its overall success rate when compared with similarly situated schools in other state district.

# Chapter Eighteen

The District's political climate begins with the National Education Association, the teachers' union (Union). This organization represents all District teachers because joining the Union is mandatory. Its major concerns include teacher pay, retirement, tenure, and fringe benefits such as vacation and sick leave. Although important, the Union does not attempt to compute teacher quality. In general the Union motto is essentially that a teacher is a teacher. Unlike unions in other districts, the Union allows Springs significant discretion in terminating teachers from positions for good cause. Although tenure is important and provides earned security, the District is very interested in teachers maintaining competency and not hurting younger teachers with budding creativity. This encouraging perspective has allowed the District to maintain its above national average rating in national standardized testing.

The Union president is Teresa Rojas, a biology teacher at Obama High School. Teresa has 22 years in the District and has an excellent working relationship with Angela. This is important because the relationship gives the Union credibility with Springs and the legislative and board members in the state and local area. If Teresa believes that an issue is very important to the Union, she is likely to prevail over any opposition.

The District's school board essentially rubberstamps Springs' mandates. The Adobe Acres School Board (Board) has five members. Two are from Northeast, two are from the Valley, and one is at large. John Smith, a former state secretary of education, is President and is a personal friend of Springs. The other four members, two male and two female, are concerned parents and generally follow Smith's lead.

The state education secretary, Juan Rosa, primarily focuses on the state budget and, with recent funding cutbacks, he emphasizes that the school districts should do more with less. The District is fortunate in its operations because of its generous sponsors. Springs sees to it that District employees are paid at above average rates, satisfying the Union, and the above average scores on standardized testing satisfies Rosa.

Ricardo Sanchez is the District's Democratic state legislator. He is also Angela's boyfriend which provides a valuable connection to favorable school legislation. Ricardo is from the Valley and an Obama High School graduate. Ricardo is chairman of the legislative education committee. He is also a first cousin to the governor. Ricardo is currently attempting to engineer a new bill which would in construction of two new elementary schools and a new high school in the Districts's economically depressed Valley.

Helen Brooks, a Republican representative whose constituents primarily occupy the Northeast, is less friendly to Springs and the District. She is a strong conservative who battles consistently with Ricardo on spending bills. Helen believes that the District is pampered by the state educational institutions and regularly brings up new bills to cut District spending. Her vote tends to cancel out Ricardo's vote.

Mannie Richardson, is the District's state senator. Mannie is a Democrat who votes strictly along party lines. As a strong supporter of the governor, He tends to favor education bills and is Ricardo's ally in the upper house. Mannie is a son of Naomi Richardson, a single mother who was among the first graduates of Grant Alternative High School. Naomi worked two jobs to insure that Mannie would have a middle class upbringing.

After graduating as a valedictorian from Obama High, Mannie received a full scholarship to Yale University. He then went on to Harvard Law School where he was the assistant editor of the Harvard Law Review. Mannie then returned to the District where he became a very successful ambulance chaser, specializing in drunk driving cases. Mannie has regular lunches with Springs and is married to Angela's older sister, Anita.

# Chapter Nineteen

Substitute services has become increasingly more important to District education. All substitute teachers are now required to have an undergraduate degree, to pass a background security screening, and to attend a District orientation. Roberta Garcia, managing the substitute teacher program, has a general philosophy that a substitute should be able to teach in place of a regular teacher as if it's a regular school day. Consistent with this philosophy, the regularly assigned teacher is required to provide the substitute with a detailed lesson plan.

Many substitutes are retired teachers looking to keep busy. Recent college graduates, still looking for full time employment, make up another large group. There is also a smaller group of career substitutes. Among this group is Annie Hodges, a single mother of five sons and three daughters, who has substituted for 15 years. Annie prefers to teach at the elementary school level where she finds her students to be enthusiastic about learning.

Roberta is concerned that the substitutes maintain a proper image and has developed a 15 page Substitute Teachers Handbook. Because there is a long list of available substitute teachers, Roberta will automatically terminate any individual who violates the disciplinary requirements contained in the handbook. She also has a three strikes policy where she will dismiss any individual who receives three adverse school reports.

The District pays substitute teachers only for days worked with no fringe benefits. The daily stipend is $75 for a full day and $50 for a partial day over one hour. If less than one hour, or the school no longer needs the substitute, the pay is $15. A majority of the teachers find this pay satisfactory because they can work their own hours and they enjoy being with the students. Substitutes with teacher certification receive an additional ten percent.

# Chapter Twenty

The District, led by Wally Springs, is fully aware of recent efforts in educational circles to increase teacher quality. This begins with a critical attack on teachers who major in education at the undergraduate level lacking subject matter expertise. These teachers, constituting the vast majority of new teachers, take far fewer courses in their field of study than individuals who major in that field. Instead they take classes such as the philosophy or history of education.

The second pipeline of new teachers, gaining in popularity, is the alternative teacher route. These teachers generally have earned degrees in their chosen field of study and have completed a teacher certification program. Adobe Acres Community College has one of these programs which requires completion of six educational courses and passing a state standard examination for certification.

District teachers are organized into gold and silver teams to insure that education at all levels maintains its cutting edge. A lead teacher at each of the District's 100 schools heads a committee which meets twice each week to review recent educational developments. The committee thoroughly researches these developments and then presents them to the school principal for further dissemination to school teachers and staff.

Should the principal believe that a particular development is worthwhile to the District as a whole, then that information is sent directly to Springs. Springs regularly instructs Angela to put this information out to the public media. Occasionally, where a significant expense may be involved, such as a new educational program or information technology development, Springs will attempt to obtain a sponsorship, usually successfully.

Parents are key to District success and are very supportive of teachers and staff. Parent-teacher conferences are an excellent tool for teachers to discuss a student's progress and are held four times each school year. Springs requires teachers to use a standard checklist to measure this progress, similarly to how a doctor would measure a patient's health. The checklist is also intended to invoke parent interaction.

The majority of parents, although expressing lip service to the checklist, are not interested in details. They merely desire to hear that their student is making satisfactory progress. When advised on steps to take to help their student, they will readily agree to do so, but unless developing the habit of helping, they fail to do so. There are many students that do not have the support of a parent or guardian and struggle without good teaching help.

Springs considers homework to be very important to student development. He cites various studies showing a direct correlation between learning and the amount of homework that a teacher assigns. District policy requires that elementary schools give two hours of homework each night with four hours on weekends. For middle and high schools, the District requires three hours each night with a minimum of six hours per weekend.

Going against some new teaching theory, Springs strongly supports rote memorization for both literacy and math. The most popular teachers tend to give the least homework. This often occurs in electives where some teachers are happy to have students attend. The strong math and literacy teachers have shown that they can increase student scores on standardized tests if students will put their best efforts forward on homework assignments.

There is a direct correlation between homework and grading. Teachers continuously rate student performance throughout the school year and issue report cards to parents at stated intervals. Most teachers use a point grading scale, with total correct points divided by total possible points to get a percentage which is translated into a grade. The District uses a standard A to F grading scale for most classes. However, in middle and high school elective classes, a pass to fail system is used.

Courses in literacy, math, and science are required at all three grade levels. Springs has initiated additional required courses in geography and physical education. Most students take an American history course as well. Elective courses are available in homemaking, economics, drama, shop, keyboarding, and band. Principals may petition Angela for other elective classes if they can establish sufficient student interest.

Each District middle school provides thirty minutes for lunch. Half of the students eat lunch in the cafeteria while half bring sack lunches or eat pizza at school provided alternative locations. Students may also purchase energy drinks, candy, or popcorn. Some middle schools worried about student health have requested that the District change its policies on lunch and provide healthy alternatives. Angela has yet to approve any changes.

Middle schools schedule student wide conferences monthly with guest speakers. These hour long conferences bring community guest speakers into the school to encourage students and to provide realistic assessments of future life activities. Guest speakers include celebrities, government officials, and sometimes teachers or other educators. These role models are considered important in providing real life experiences to students.

# Chapter Twenty-One

There are certain elective courses which do not require homework. These include keyboarding, drivers education, lifestyle experiences, and shop. However, the more recent trend is to put more classes into the common core of math, literacy, and science. Drivers education is extremely popular and has been around for decades. One of the urban legends involves a homecoming queen at Obama High who ran over a grandmother who had fallen to her knees in a crosswalk two blocks from school.

Certification of teachers at all levels is continuously under attack. This is particularly true in math and science. Middle school math teachers may have difficulty in understanding algebra and geometry. Math high school teachers fare somewhat better, but still lack advanced math acumen. Science teachers suffer from the same watered down process. Although biology and chemistry are taught at basic levels, the teacher may only be qualified to teach the more generalized category of science appreciation.

This more watered down category may well apply to the school psychologist. About one fourth of these staff members have an advanced psychology degree while the others fit more into a category of educational specialist. Nonetheless parents trust these professionals to advise them on the future of their children. This lack of challenge to those who do not have the education and experience of your child psychologist may bring adverse results.

No wonder there is a growing movement to charter schools, home schooling, and school vouchers. Generally these vouchers may be used at private or parochial schools. This option is not generally available yet, but Republicans keep pushing for it. There may be residual costs to the parents and transportation may well be an issue. However, the NCLB law which requires schools to meet annual yearly progress or face severe consequences makes it less favorable.

Charter schools and home schooling are other options to public schools. Charter schools get away from the standardized bureaucracy, but usually are funded at lower levels and have inferior equipment and buildings. This is particularly true in the District where Springs has been successful in obtaining sponsorship for school programs. The District has five charter schools which are somewhat specialized. All five schools run from kindergarten through twelfth grades. The average student population at these schools is 500.

Home schooling in the District is parent driven. Students have shown surprisingly good results when taking required standardized testing. Somewhat socially isolated, the charter schools invite these students to their events and allow them equal access to sporting events and other extracurricular activities. Teachers tend to earn lower salaries in these alternative options to the public school system.

One of the advantages of charter schools is that they employ a greater percentage of teachers who received alternative teacher certificates. These teachers tend to be ten years older on average than educational majors. They have more experience and many of them come from special areas such as the military's Troop to Teachers program. In general there is a higher percentage of males than females from these programs.

# Chapter Twenty-Two

Private schools have the advantage of hiring teachers and keeping those considered best without seniority considerations. The two private schools in the District, Adobe Acres Academy and Northeast Heights Preparatory School, are kindergarten through twelfth grade schools with a high tuition cost. Northeast Heights is patterned after the Knowledge is Power Program (KIPP) and receives significant financial support from wealthy supporters.

KIPP is a nationwide network of preparatory schools scattered throughout communities in the United States. These schools, usually established under state charter school laws, is headquartered in San Francisco. Northeast Heights has attracted some of these KIPP teachers to Northeast Heights at significant premium salaries. This is an unusual example of a school with rich student families duplicating a program used in poorer communities.

Each school has a Parent Teachers Association (PTA). These parents are loyal adjuncts to the teachers. This respect comes from the respect that a parent holds for the teacher as an authority figure. The teachers encourage this authority by tasking parents to help their students with their homework and certain school social activities. Parent support is strongest in the Valley schools.

The PTA is not as docile in the District's Northeast schools. Higher income and better educated parents are more demanding of teacher quality. The PTAs for the elementary schools tend to be the most vocal. They will go directly to Springs for relief and are usually successful in bringing change. One parent, Lucy Livermore, complained that the media center at Quincy Elementary School was inferior to one she had visited in New York. She started a fundraising campaign, with Springs' blessing, which raised $70,000 for a major renovation.

The District School Board (Board) has five members. Donald Lucas, from Northeast, is chairman. He is one of Springs' best friends and lives on the same city street. Donald is easily reelected every four years in an election where forty percent of his board district votes. The other four members are easily led by Donald, but will occasionally fight him on issues that the Union deems detrimental to District teachers.

The state legislature determines the District's budget for school construction. Prior to the recent economic downturn, several million dollars were allocated to the building of three new elementary schools, two new middle schools, and a new general high school. These projects were cancelled and a reduced amount was then allocated to school renovations.

# Chapter Twenty-Three

Grade inflation tends to be a District problem. Parents love their student to get great grades and hold teachers responsible when the student fails to meet expectations. Under the current perspective, an A means above average work, a B means average work, and grades below B tend to be unacceptable. Parents routinely place bumper stickers on cars heralding "honor student on board."

Springs emails the Superintendents Message to parents weekly. This message advises parents of the wonderful activities currently ongoing in District schools. Sports activities and extracurricular activities are prominent. Springs also includes school open houses, math and science competitions, club news, and Board meetings. The message also contains stories on the teacher and student of the week.

District kindergartens focus on what Springs calls a good start. These classes are limited to no more than fifteen students. Each class has both an educational assistant for the teacher and a grandma.

Additionally each student is requested to bring a parent of the week to class for more individualized attention. Springs objective is to have each student read and write at an above average level at the end of the school year.

In the 20 middle schools, Springs has initiated a physics and geography program. All students in the seventh grade are required to take a geography class and all eighth grade students are required to take a physics class. These requirements have resulted in students scoring significantly above national average in standardized science testing.

District bullies come in all shapes and sizes. Elementary school bullies are typically overgrown mean slow learners. Both boys and girls qualify. These students hit others, but when hit by another student are the first to tattle. Middle school bullies, usually boys, have no interest in learning. Mean girls in high school make fun out of any other young women that are different from normal which often include being overweight or dressing poorly.

Young men in high school, apart from those that have failed or stopped attending, general will outgrow bullying. These students are more likely to engage in criminal behavior such as drug dealing and associated offenses. At some point these men will either graduate or move on to other pursuits.

# Chapter Twenty-Four

There is a generalized student handbook which contains District disciplinary policies as well as general information and contact numbers. This handbook is supplemented by individual schools for local information. Angela has the responsibility for maintaining consistency and reviews this handbook annually with selected help from other District personnel.

The District policy on calling home is very liberal. School staff often do this for many reasons. First calls are for daily absences where a recorded message is left. If less than three days, a parental slip is required. Students absent for three days or more must bring in a doctor's excuse. If a student is absent for two weeks or longer, the District contacts child protective services for intervention.

Teachers keep good records on emergency cards for each student and will regularly telephone home if an issue arises. Parent response is mixed with some parents showing significant concern while others provide little response. In reality, both parent and teacher know that student behavior is problematic. The teacher is left to search for a solution while the parent hope that there will be no consequences. Consequences may come later when there is a law enforcement solution.

District high schools interface with the local Sagebrush Community College system. High school seniors are allowed to take classes and obtain credit for basic freshman classes in literacy and math at the college. This head start may be transferred to most American colleges and universities. The sole limitation on these credits is that they are not eligible for the student's concentration or major.

Dances are a form of extracurricular activity at the middle and high schools gaining in popularity, spurred on by the multitude of dance programs on television. This is particularly true of high school prom night. For many young women, this is the most important night of the high school experience. For too many of them, this is the night of lost virtue. For many young men, this is the night of their first conquest.

# Chapter Twenty-Five

The American dream for Springs is to have his state win the race to the top. This national program provides millions of dollars annually to states where its schools perform best. This program unleashed forces that had been pent up for years under the general philosophy that a teacher is just a teacher and fully interchangeable. Given the money involved, many states put this race front and center.

Springs' focus on teacher quality is consistent with the modern trend in education arena. Over the past six decades, the public perception is that the American public school system has deteriorated markedly. This is why statistically the USA finds itself 25th in the world in math and science despite the highest per student spending rate. Springs has identified the District's motto as "improving the potential" and works hard to do so. Of course, having an attractive media alert vice-superintendent, as Angela surely is, helps his efforts.

# Chapter Twenty-Six

The District obtains its financing through federal, state, local, and private aid. Federal regulations such as NCLB have usurped what used to be local control. Springs has welcomed and sought to fashion District policies faced on this assistance. Property taxes continue to be a major source of financing, but under current practice, the standardized testing scores are the single most important criteria for success.

The Union is supportive of District policies only because of its success. Teachers obtaining tenure must still produce or they will be terminated for cause. Unlike metropolitan areas like New York City, the District does not maintain a deadbeats list. The District's push for quality education is attracting teachers across the nation with many new teachers coming from programs such as Teach for America and Troops to Teachers.

Seniority remains important as seen in the District's July ritual. Teachers may request retention at their service schools and most do. However, they may apply for any District open teaching position they are qualified for. Once these positions are filled, Springs doles out any remaining vacancies to new teachers. Springs also will fill any special positions with program teachers from Teach for America or related positions.

The federal NCLB regulations have a significant impact on District school operations. This law requires schools to show annual yearly progress or suffer the consequences. These consequences within a five year sequential period of failure include termination of teachers and staff and the closing of the failing school itself.

The general impact of NCLB has had a twofold impact within the District. Initially the state lowered academic standards to reduce the passing bar. Secondly, highly qualified teachers required within NCLB spend a significant amount of time teaching to the test. This standardized test is administered each year to third through eighth graders and once during the high school years.

NCLB focuses on four areas of study: reading, language arts, mathematics, and science. Springs has of course increased hours in these subjects at the expense of special elective subjects such as history, music, and art. Although several schools in the Valley have failed to show annual yearly progress, Springs is adroit at placing new teachers and staff at these schools to improve results. No District school has failed to make progress for more than two years.

# Chapter Twenty-Seven

Consistent with test standardization, the common core has taken over the curriculum at elementary schools. The basic idea is to have standardization in reading and math to improve overall test scores on standardized testing. Although this has brought about some improvement in scoring, the process is in early stage development.

Although not currently present in the District, there are parental efforts to take over failing schools in poorly performing school districts throughout the United States and particularly in California. For example, recently in the Compton, California, school jurisdiction, parents have determined that the school is more interested in serving the interests of the adult teachers and administration than in serving the interests of the students. Springs is well aware of the potential adverse consequences for the District and receives high marks from community activists who really believe that the District puts student interests first.

Moreover, New Jersey's governor Christie is fighting teacher unions in an effort to improve quality education in his state. Recent developments establish the difficulty of this movement. However, despite its watered down nature which includes more due process rights than originally contemplated, the new law makes tenure harder to get and firings easier to be carried out. Springs believes that the District is ahead of the curve in this area because his policies currently bypass seniority and quickly dispose of new teachers.

There is another option available to struggling school districts with high teacher salaries and students failing standardized testing. This option, currently in process in Michigan, involves outsourcing to private enterprises. Highland Park School District is turning over its poorly performing schools to a for profit charter school company. This devastated surrounding community will pay about $7,000 per student which allows for the school's professional staff to receive about half of the pay previously spent. This is done under an emergency law.

Furthermore, in an increasingly diverse society some schools are now finding that teachers are dressing inappropriately in jeans, skinny straps, and with body piercings. The Wichita School District is cracking down on such dress and, in Arizona, the state is setting a business casual dress requirement. Springs is taking note of this movement and is using Angela as an example of appropriate dress. Angela is using her public affairs skills to publicize the advantage and professionalism of a typical business dress code.

# Chapter Twenty-Eight

Springs takes a stronger approach to inappropriate conduct between teacher and student and is constantly looking out for inappropriate behavior. Springs points to attitudes in New York City as a base line. For example, a recent Wall Street Journal article stated that its system is rigged so that abusive teachers who may be sexual predators are allowed to stay in the classroom. The opposite is true in the District where an allegation of any teacher misconduct will result in the automatic suspension of a teacher until resolution.

New York City does serve as a positive example in its success schools. Recently these charter schools, despite its poverty underlining, outperformed the public schools by an average of over 7 points in math. This is made possible by a system in which the teachers work hard, are better compensated than other public school teachers, and move on if unable to meet rigorous evaluation standards. These teachers truly thrive in an atmosphere where success receives reward and mediocrity is not tolerated. Springs believes that this focus on success is taking hold in the District.

The modern trend for success can and does result in data abuses as in Atlanta and recently alleged in Ohio where the Ohio Auditor of State has launched a statewide probe into allegations that several school districts fudged student data to improve academic standing. As found in a District elementary school, the staff was sanctioned and the school's reputation tarnished. Springs terminated the principal and promoted the vice-principal who had been the initial whistle blower.

# CONCLUSION

The District under the guidance of Springs and Angela, and its supporting cast of teachers and staff, striving for excellence embraces the modern trend of quality education and breaks the mold of the philosophy that a "teacher is a teacher is a teacher." This approach is high on cost-benefit analysis. The restrictions and regulations placed on most school districts is relaxed because all of the involved constituents, including the teacher's union, are focused on insuring that each student receives a quality education and not other vested interests.

In the modern American Public School System, the District stands out as a shining example on the hill. I believe that the elements which will lead our children into the future as accountable and responsible adults are present everywhere and, like a green plant, needs only the appropriate measure of nourishment. Thank you for reading this book.

# ABOUT THE AUTHOR

Dennis Wallace is a retired Army Lawyer who has spent the past seven years teaching in the Albuquerque, New Mexico, public school system (best known as APS). Prior to writing this book, Mr. Wallace served as an Administrative Attorney for the Albuquerque District Corps of Engineers for twelve years. He then spent two years obtaining teacher certification in New Mexico before his employment in APS. Mr. Wallace also serves as an adjunct professor at the University of New Mexico.

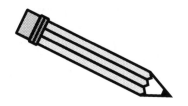